windows

architectural details

Imprint
The Deutsche Bibliothek is registering
this publication in the Deutsche
Nationalbibliographie; detailed
bibliographical information can be found
on the internet at http://dnb.ddb.de

ISBN 978-3-938780-37-4 (Hardcover)
ISBN 978-3-938780-42-8 (Softcover)

© 2008 by Verlagshaus Braun
www.verlagshaus-braun.de

1st edition 2008

Editor:
Markus Sebastian Braun
Editorial staff:
Susanne Laßwitz
Translation:
Alice Bayandin, María José Garibotto
Graphic concept and layout:
Michaela Prinz
Reproduction:
LVD Gesellschaft für Datenverarbeitung
mbH, Berlin

windows

architectural details

BRAUN

contents

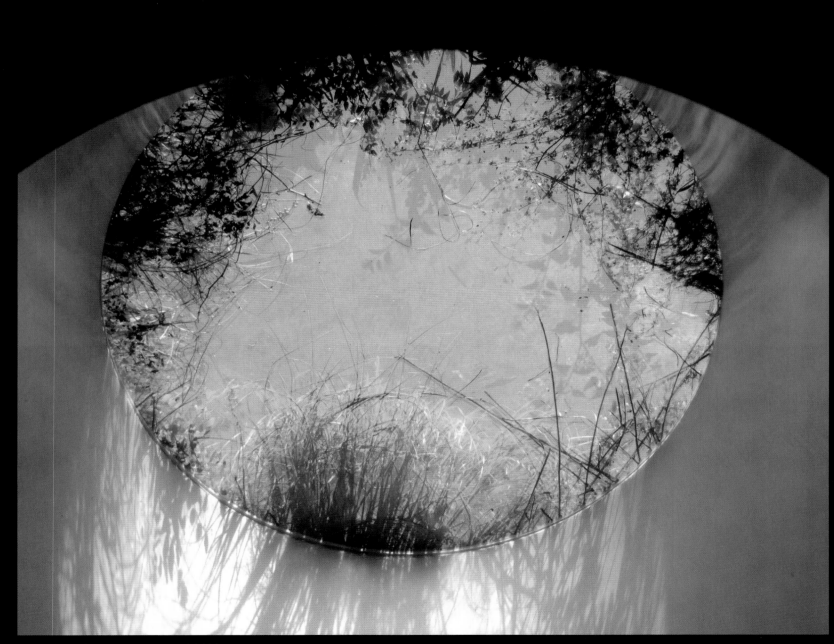

zurich, plattenstrasse 14/20

windows – framing a view

"Windows are the eyes to the house, as the eye is a window to the soul. Therefore Slavs have built directly their "oko" eye, as their "okno" window…" This was written in 1854 in *Grimm'sches Wörterbuch* (*Grimm's Dictionary*). As an opening in the wall, windows are an essential means of "eye" contact between the internal and external world that function in both directions: they permit light and air to move through the room or building, and they also enable one to look outside. In the same way, with the exception of the usual frosted glass used in many bathrooms, windows provide a view of the inside and, therefore, give way to the invasion of intimacy. Occupants constantly try to exercise control over this visual relationship using curtains, drapes, shutters, blinds as well as other resources.

The current *Encyclopaedia Britannica* introduces windows as follows: "opening in the wall of a building for the admission of light and air and sometimes for framing a view; windows are often arranged also for the purposes of architecture decoration. Since early times, the opening has been filled with stone, wooden or iron grilles or lights (panes) of glass or other translucent material such as mica or, in the Far East, paper". Then, some window types are explained briefly: "A window in a vertically sliding is called a sash window: a single-hang sash has only one half that moves; in a double-hung sash, both parts slide. A casement window swings open on hinges attached to the upright side of the frame. Awning windows swing outward on hinges attached to the top of the frame; hopper windows swing inward on hinges attached to the bottom of the frame. Large, fixed (non-operating) areas of glass are commonly called picture windows. A bay window is an exterior projection of a bay of a building that also forms on interior recess, providing better light and view than would a window flush with the building line".

Of course, it also refers to special types of windows, such as the "oeil-de-boeuf window": "also called bull's eye window; in architecture, a small circular or oval window, usually resembling a wheel, glazing bars (bars framing the panes of glass) as spokes radiating outward from an empty hub, or circular center. In French, oeil-de-boeuf means "eye of the steer", and, in the French chateau of Versailles, erected for Louis XIV between 1661 and 1708, there is a small antechamber called the oeil-de-boeuf…".

The German word "Fenster" is derived from the Latin word "fenestra", whereas the English term "window" is a modification of the Gothic word "windauga" (wind-eye).

Modern windows consist of glass panes framed in wood or aluminum, though there are also glass façades in post and rail façades. The earlier style of constructing buildings as blockhouse or timbered houses with waffle-like construction promoted the rectangular window form that prevails even today. Special care was given to the completion of the upper window in the wall - the lintel -, which was finished in weatherproof wood or brick, nowadays of steel or concrete, due to the fact that the load forces of the wall needed to be conducted around the window. Especially in medieval, Romantic and Gothic times, windows were therefore small. Rounded or pointed arches were used to withstand the load of brickwork and wider glassed façades which usually consisted of many consecutive arched windows, divided and stabilized by arches or columns.

A playful element in window design appeared in the Gothic period, in which the top point was decorated with rosettes and vegetable or geometric constructions. In addition, stained glass panels depicting representations of saints or religious scenes were used to bring life into church windows. During the Renaissance, supporting structures were made slender; columns and arches were replaced by brick crosses (cross windows). Furthermore, flexible lead was used for window design, especially for small bull's eye panes. In addition, windows were made from several pieces of glass that brought life to glass façades, while at the same time hindering the view inside.

After many decorative window designs during the Baroque and Rococo eras and with the advent of civil culture, the soberly functional window design that included the simple glass front appeared. With the arrival of heat engineering and noise protection, the simple window was replaced by laminated isolating glazing which improved its isolating properties. Currently, there are two different types of double windows that consist of individual window fronts located one after the other but in one type they can be operated separately (double casement window) whereas in the other type they are linked with each other in one construction (double-glazed window). Depending on how the window is opened two types of windows can be conceived: single-sash windows, in which the whole window can be moved in one way, and casement windows that usually have two parallel sashes that can be moved separately. The superior horizontal parts of a window are for ventilation, which can be opened totally or partly.

Current articles on windows are generally as simple as the function of windows itself. Luckily there are some exceptions. A look at older reference books sometimes promotes some curious knowledge about the idea of windows and their cultural history. In the article "Fenster" (windows) that appeared in 1773 in the *Oekonomische Encyclopaedie* (*Economic Encyclopedia*) of Johann Georg Krünitz the following is written regarding the aesthetic function rather than the architectural purpose: "Windows are necessary for comfort, but can also serve as adornment for a building whose exterior is not adorned with columns or arches and would therefore have a cold appearance if the monotony were not discontinued by the skilful distribution of windows". We also learn that there are "window-rights", namely "the liberties granted to windows in different rights are that one is not allowed to ruin the light of the other … are called the right to windows or to lights". In connection with rights and windows, Krünitz refers to the old bad habits of using windows as comfortable dustbins through which people could throw everything outside.

The strong penalties established by Romans against this bad habit seem not to have been of any help, as the article then observes: "This careless and thoughtless procedure that is still tolerated in many places, especially in university towns, and that results in streets and lanes to be filled with chamber pots and filth, causes many injuries and damages to pedestrians, especially at night and if they ignore the usual shouts of warning coming from people engaging in such behavior".

In the article on windows, the *Grimm's Dictionary* traces the expressions and sayings related to the term "window". The definition of window reads: "Window means an opening, hole, the cavity on the wall through which day breaks in and through which the house can look outside: to give alms to the beggar through the window, to throw money through the window … the day breaks in through the windows".
Then, the Brothers Grimm studied the use of the word window in many Bible passages - Genesis 8:6 about the Flood: "After forty days, Noah opened the window and let a raven fly away". In the German epics of the Middle Ages and in many expressions of the early modern times, for example, when Johann Wiganda (*Ob die newen Wittenberger*, 1575) says: "To the love of God, because it is not blind but he sees all the children through the blue windows".
With special delight, the article turns to human properties that are linked to windows and seem to appear at all times or at least before the implementation of cell phones.
In accordance with their own time, the Brothers Grimm give a specific gender-related description: "to look through the window, to stand by the window, to lean on the window" refer to yearning, curiosity, otiose women. The "existence by the window" is seen as a female bad habit and many of the old sayings containing the word "window" and

that have now fallen into disuse were used to refer to gossipy laziness. As an example of other bad habits related to windows, the dictionary mentions the painful fact that "windows are an ideal passage that allows prisoners to escape and burglars to come in…".

However, we learn something else about the history of window panes as we know them today: "Window panes, that were unknown to ancient times, were established in the course of time; in the past people used grids or pre-stressed linen, in the same way that paper is sometimes used nowadays". And how do we refer to windowpanes? "We say that the window warms up and perspires, creates flowers out of frost and defrosts."
To conclude, another saying of the Brothers Grimm that shows that many times building constructors do not enjoy their own work, especially the well-deserved view through their own windows. It also serves as consolation for all those who inherit houses with windows: "If you build a house, then another will look at the window from the outside".

Markus Hattstein

amsterdam

above left, below left, right: amsterdam, zwanenburgwal 2 | peter cornelius hoofstraat 47 | haarlemmerstraat 124 (posthoornkerk)

BOSS
HUGO BOSS

12

amsterdam, hoogte kadijk

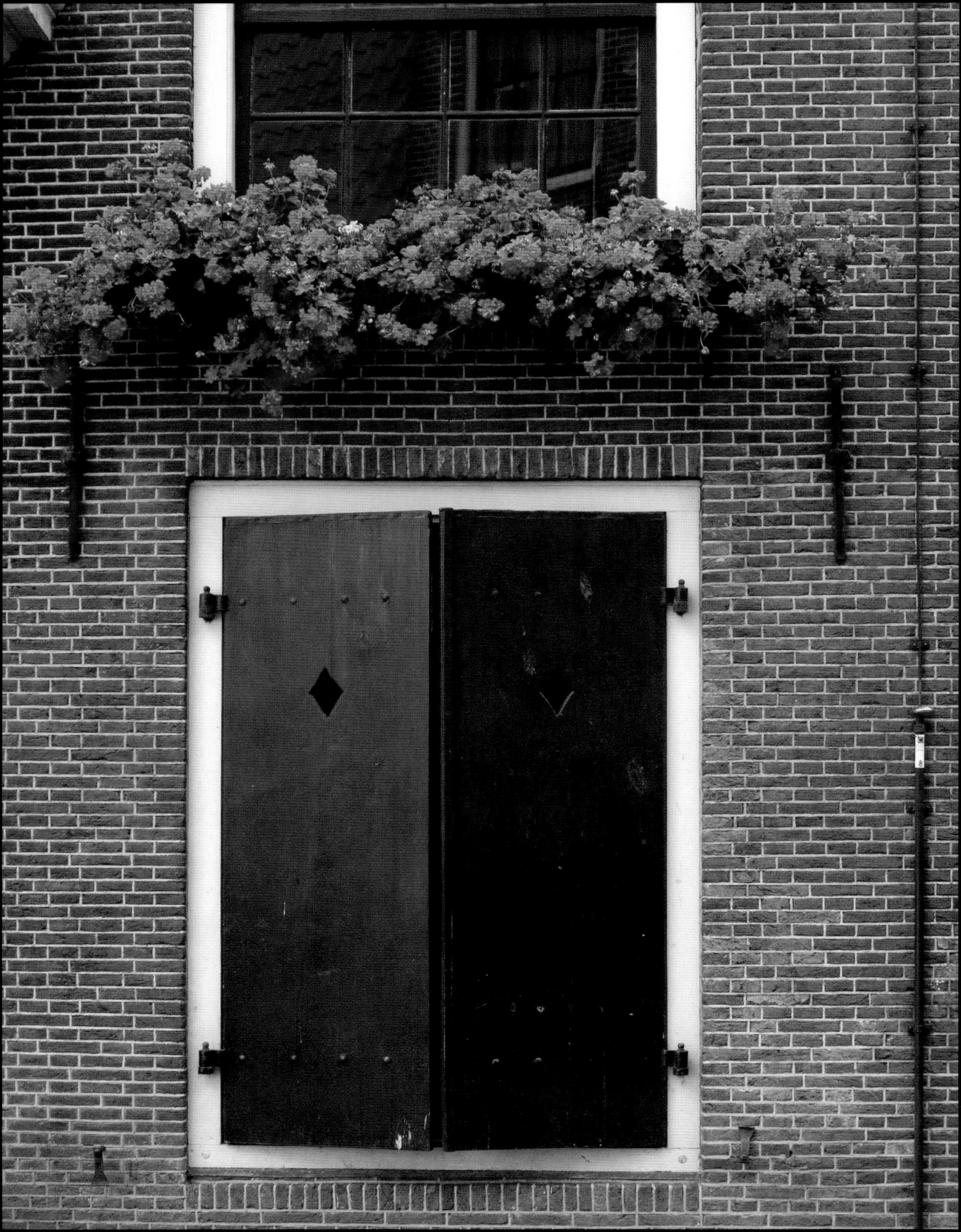

amsterdam, oudekerksplein 23 (oude kerk)

athens

athens, akti kondyli

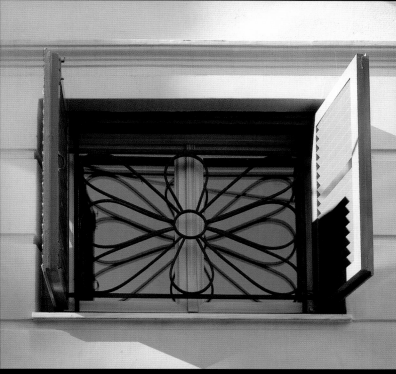

athens, korai 5

athens, akropolis

above left, above right, below left, below right: athens, ermou (kapnikarea) | ermou (kapnikarea) | kladou 9 |

anafiotika 4

barcelona

barcelona, avenida marquès de comillas 13 (poble español de montjuïc)

above left, below left, right: barcelona, plaza del tibidabo 1 (temple expiatori del sagrat cor) | plaza del tibidabo 1 (temple expiatori del sagrat cor) | calle mallorca 401 (sagrada família)

24

barcelona, calle mallorca 401 (sagrada família)

barcelona, avenida marquès de comillas 13 (poble español de montjuïc)

above left, above right, below left, below right: barcelona, rambla de sant josep 51-59 (gran teatre del liceu) |

passeig de gràcia 45 | plaza del rei 2 (palau reial) | calle mallorca 401 (sagrada família)

above left, below left, mid, right: barcelona, carrer d'olot 7 (parc güell) | passeig de gràcia 92 (casa milà) |
calle sant pau 34 | carrer d'olot 7 (parc güell)

berlin, klingelhöfer straße 21 (chinesisches kulturzentrum)

above left, above right, below left, below right: berlin, rosenthaler straße 30 | marlene-dietrich-platz 2

(hyatt berlin) | schönhauser allee | hiroshimastraße 17 (friedrich-ebert-stiftung) above left, above right, below left, below right: berlin, klingelhöferstraße | herbert-von-karajan-straße 1 (philharmonie) | hiroshimastraße 24 (landesvertretung bremen) | potsdamer straße 33 (staatsbibliothek)

berlin, hinter dem gießhaus / unter den linden 2 (deutsches historisches museum)

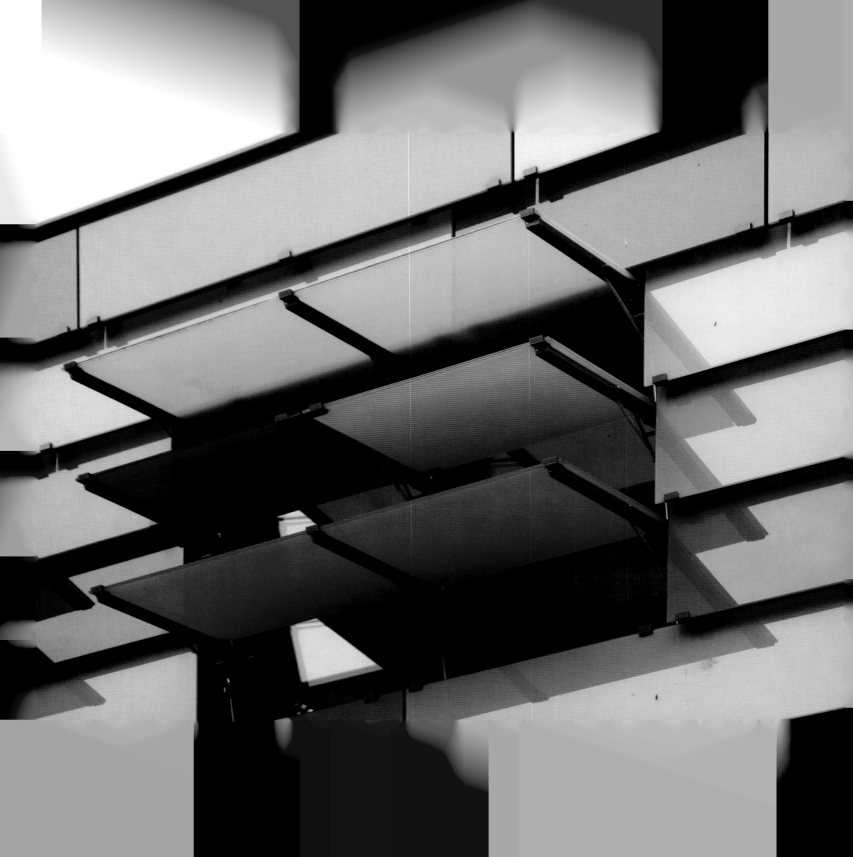

above left, above right, below left, below right: berlin, pariser platz 6 | pariser platz 6 | christburger

straße 26 | auguststraße 26a

above left, above mid, below left, below mid, right: berlin, hinter dem gießhaus / unter den linden 2 (deutsches historisches museum) | hiroshimastraße 18 (botschaft der vereinigten arabischen emirate) | willy-brandt-straße 1 (bundeskanzleramt) | welserstraße 2 | lindenstraße 9–14 (jüdisches museum)

brussels

brussels, parc du cinquantenaire

left, above right, below right: brussels: grand place | place sainte gudule | place de la bourse

above left, above right, below left, below right: brussels, 22, grasmarkt | 3, rue de bordeaux | 16, quai aux briques | 36, rue de la bourse

brussels, 12, quai aux briques

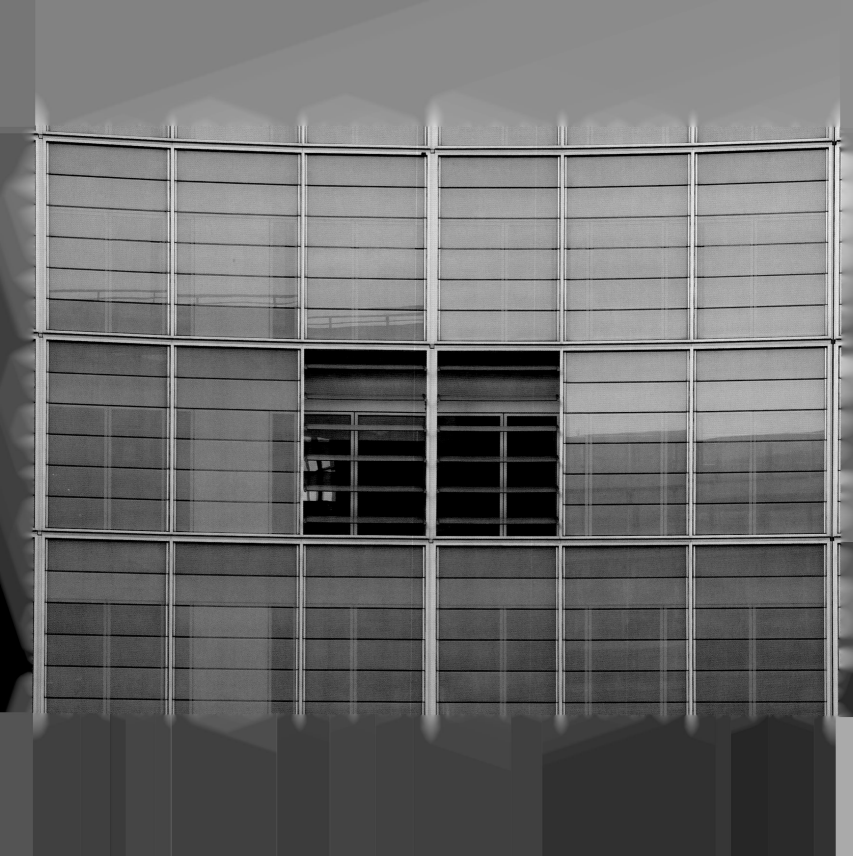

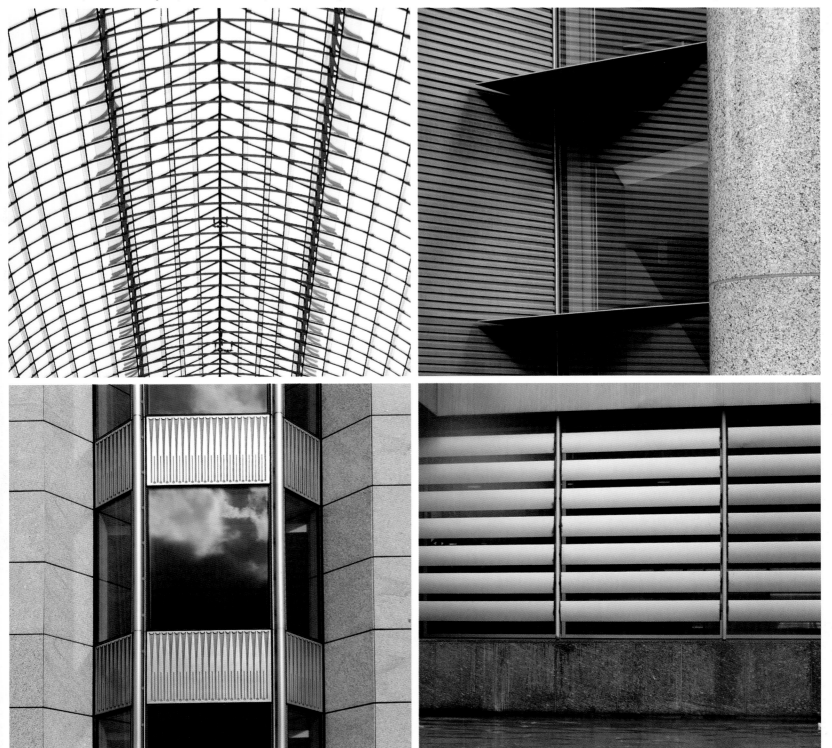

brussels, 12, avenue des gaulois

budapest

budapest, uri utca 17

budapest, állatkerti krt. 6-12 (zoo)

millenáris park

copenhagen, h. c. andersen boulevard 10

copenhagen, christians brygge 50

cracow, podzamcze 17

above left, above right, below left, below right: cracow, aleja krasińskiego 9 | rynek główny 2 | ulica estery 18 | ulica marsz. j. piłsudskiego 32

cracow, maly rynek 8

above left, above right, below left, below right: cracow, plac nowy 23 | ulica miodowa 1 | ulica marsz.
j. pilsudskiego 30 | ulica kopernika 16

cracow, ulica wielopole 6

helsinki

helsinki, mannerheimaukio

helsinki, hammarskjöldintie

aleksanterinkatu

above left, above mid, below left, below mid, right: helsinki, johnstenberginranta | ratakatu | ratakatu | ratakatu | itäinenpapinkatu | ratakatu

istanbul

istanbul, istiklal caddesi

above left, above right, below left, below right: istanbul, tavukhane sokak | h'davendigar caddesi | divanyolu caddesi | h'davendigar caddesi

HOTEL AMISOS

ŞEHIT OSMAN BATUK HAN

istanbul, tavukhane sokak

lisbon

lisbon, parque das nações (parque expo 98)

above left, above right, below left, below right: lisbon, parque das nações (parque expo 98) | avenida fontes
pereira de melo 13 | parque das nações (parque expo 98) | avenida da república 67

lisbon, avenida da liberdade 173

lisbon, praça do imperio (mosteiro dos jerónimos)

above left, above right, below left, below right: lisbon, avenida da república 38a | igreja de santa maria major | praça do imperio (mosteiro dos jerónimos) | praça dom loco da cama 7

left, above mid, below mid, right: lisbon, avenida fontes pereira de melo 9 | parque das nações (parque expo 98) | rua do jasmin | avenida fontes pereira de melo 9

84

ljubljana

ljubljana, tabor 4

above left, above right, below left, below right: ljubljana, riharjeva ulica 17 | krakovska ulica 21 |

aškerčeva ulica 5 | rožna ulica

left, above right, below right: ljubljana, gruberjeva palača | kopitarjeva ulica 2 | tavčarjeva ulica 8a

ljubljana, vodnikov trg 6

london

london, 42 cornhill street

london, 28 shad thames, buttler's wharf (design museum)

london, 87-135 brompton road (harrods)

fields (sir john soanes museum) | piccadilly circus (the criterion theatre)

left, above mid, below mid, right: london, 195-197 kings road | 79/81 portobello road | 13 lincoln's inn fields (sir john soanes museum) | covent garden market

paris, esplanade de la défense (tour ariane)

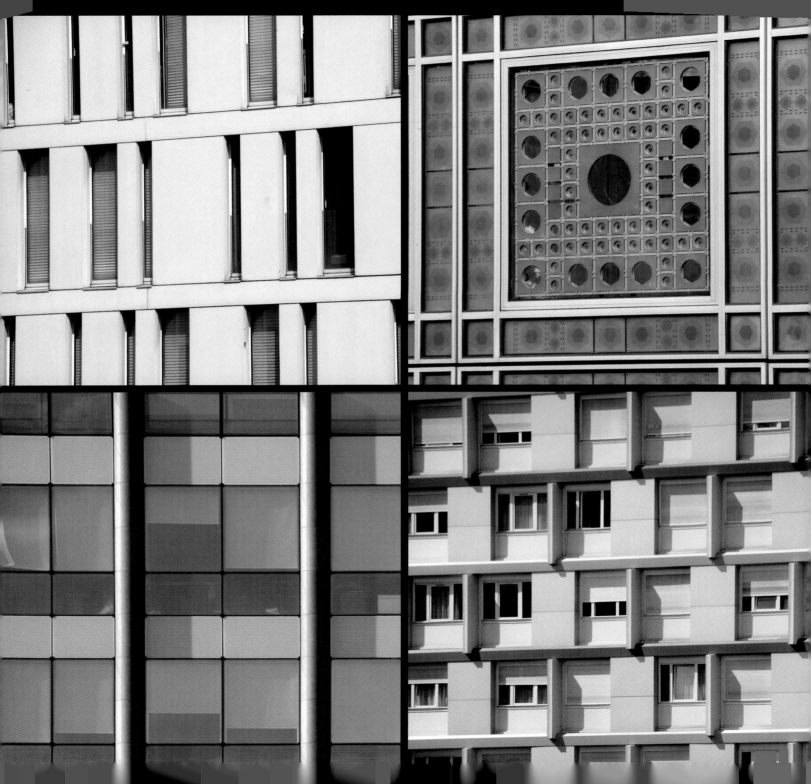

left, above right, below right: paris, église de montmatre | 4 place jussieu | esplanade de la défense

paris, 4 place jussieu

paris, 35 rue du chevalier de la barre (basilique du sacré-cœur de montmartre)

above left, above right, below left, below right: paris, place du parvis (notre-dame) | 21 rue des abbesses |

place du parvis (notre-dame) | 5 rue gabrielle

above left, above mid, below left, below mid, right: paris, 39 rue de la bucherie | 22 rue du cloitre | 10 rue thenard | rue des abbesses / rue andre antoine | 21 rue de lyon

prague

prague, schwarzenbersky palac

prague, rasinovo nabrezi 80

prague, jirska 2

zlata ulicka 24

riga

riga, lomonosova ielā

above left, above right, below left, below right: riga, kronvalda bulvāris 2 (latvijas nacionālais teātris) | mednieku ielā | jurmala | jurmala

riga, jurmala

riga, elisabetes ielā

rome

rome, via del poggio laurentino 2

above left, above right, below left, below right: rome, piazza della rotonda 116 (pantheon) | viale vatic

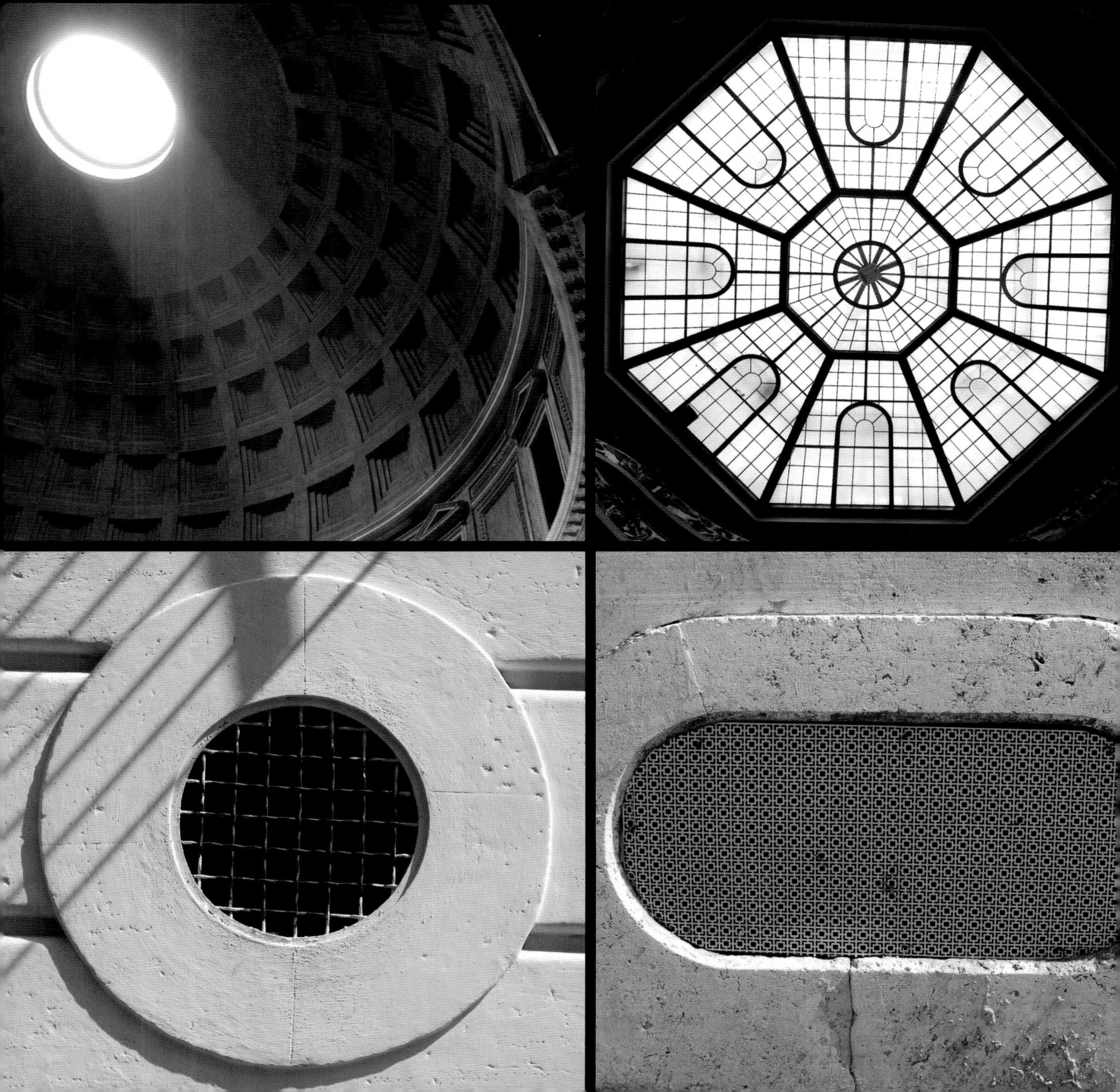

rome, viale della civiltà del lavoro (palazzo della civiltà del lavoro)

above left, above right, below left, below right: rome, piazza farnèse (palazzo farnèse) | fontana di trevi | piazza farnèse (palazzo farnèse) | viale vaticano (musei vaticani)

rome, via bocca di leon 42

stockholm

stockholm, jakobs torg (jakobskyrka)

stockholm, hötorget 8 (konserthuset)

stockholm, bondegatan

klippgatan 18

above left, above right, below left, below right: stockholm, riddarholmen (rosenhaneska palatset) | riddarholmen (riddarholmskyrkan) | eriksbergsgatan 30 | stortorget

stockholm, drottninggatan 33 (stadshuset)

st. petersburg

left, above right, below right: st. petersburg, krasnoarmeijskaja ulitsa 7 | glavnyi shtab |

malaja konjuschennaja ulitsa 7

above left, above right, below left, below right: st. petersburg, malaja konjuschennaja ulitsa 5 |
ulitsa egorova 16 | nab. reki fontanki 14 | nevskij prospekt 41

st. petersburg, malaja konjuschennaja ulitsa 5

st. petersburg, nevskij prospekt 54

rossiiskaya natsionalnaya biblioteka | karavannaja ulitsa 10

vienna

vienna, kegelergasse / löwengasse (hunderwasserhaus)

vienna, fleischmarkt 13

augustiner straße 1

vilnius

vilnius, daukanto gatvė 3

zurich

zurich, airport zurich-kloten

above left, above right, below left, below right: zurich, hardturmstrasse 11 | oranja strasse 6 | schiffbaustrasse 4 | tannenstrasse 5

zurich, paradeplatz 8

plattenstrasse 14/20 | universität zürich-zentrum (uzz)

photographers index

dominik butzmann   helsinki
www.dbutzmann.de

"what a dream – to wander the streets without a map, without a schedule and collect impressions, colors, faces, light and shadow!"

marius flucht   amsterdam, berlin
www.herrflucht.de

"look!"

katja hoffmann   ljubljana, london, vilnius
www.katjahoffmann.de

"without my camera I would have given up wanting to understand the world."

jörn hustedt   copenhagen
www.hustedtnetwork.de

"photography for me is holding still of everything subject to constant change."

thomas kierok   barcelona, vienna, zurich
www.kierok.de

"seeing is the way to awareness."

johannes kramer   athens, budapest, prague
johannes.kramer@berlin.de

**"photography for me is a confrontation with reality –
an interplay between objectivity and fantasy."**

marion lammersen   paris
www.marionlammersen.com

**"symbiosis of art and nature creates authentic and interesting
architecture."**

bernhardt link   istanbul, rome
www.link-foto.de

**"photographs reveal their own reality, or that, what the
photographer considers as such."**

kai senf   brussels
www.kaisenf.com

"the organization and engineering of any architecture I perceive
in my viewfinder suggests a feeling of order that contrasts
the storm that is going on in my head. architecture photography
has a very meditative and calming effect on me."

claudia schülke   st. petersburg
www.cs-fotodesign.com

"to photograph something you need time.
if you don't have time, you can make snapshots."

claudia weidemann   berlin, lisbon, riga, stockholm
c.weidemann@berlin.de

"photography changes my perception of reality."

katja zimmermann   cracow
office@beta-75.com

"architecture itself carries stories out of the
centuries past behind the façades – photographs of
architecture tell us completely new stories."